PACEMAKER®

Pre-Algebra

WORKBOOK

GLOBE FEARON
Pearson Learning Group

Pacemaker® Pre-Algebra Second Edition

We thank the following educators, who provided valuable comments
and suggestions during the development of the first edition of this book.

REVIEWERS

Melissa Bartolameolli (Curth), Math Teacher, Athens High School, Troy, MI 48098
Jim Geske, Math Special Ed. Chairmain, Apple Valley High School, Apple Valley, MN 55124
Lois Lanyard, Resource Center Teacher, Woodbridge High School, Woodbridge, NJ 07095

PROJECT STAFF

Executive Editor: Eleanor Ripp
Supervising Editor: Stephanie Petron Cahill
Lead Editor: Phyllis Dunsay
Editor: Theresa McCarthy
Production Editor: Travis Bailey
Lead Designer: Susan Brorein
Market Manager: Douglas Falk
Cover Design: Susan Brorein, Jennifer Visco
Editorial, Design, and Production Services: GTS Graphics
Electronic Composition: Phyllis Rosinsky

About the Cover: Pre-algebra helps people get ready for algebra. The images on the cover represent
some of the things you will be learning about in this book. The stopwatch is for measuring time.
The line graph is for showing data visually. Balancing a scale reminds us of how we balance an
equation. The hot air balloons and snowflakes remind us of positive and negative numbers. What
other images can you think of to represent pre-algebra?

ISBN: 0-130-23635-7

Printed in the United States of America

6 7 8 9 10   04

Globe Fearon
Pearson Learning Group

1-800-321-3106
www.pearsonlearning.com

Contents

A Note to the Student

The exercises in this workbook go along with your *Pacemaker® Pre-Algebra* textbook. This workbook gives you the opportunity to review concepts, practice skills, and think critically.

Set goals for yourself and try to meet them as you complete each activity. The more you practice, the more you will remember. Being able to remember and apply information is an important skill, and leads to success on tests, in school, at work, and in life.

Your critical thinking skills will be challenged. You will need to think beyond what you learned in your textbook. The critical thinking activities provide you with the opportunity to put the information you have learned to use.

Your textbook is a wonderful source of knowledge. By completing the activities in this workbook, you will learn a great deal about pre-algebra skills. The real value of the information will come when you have mastered these skills and put critical thinking to use.

Name _____ Date _____

1 ▸ Working with Whole Numbers　　　　Exercise 1

Lessons 1.1 to 1.3

A. Write the value of 8 in each number.

    1. 38,426 _____   **2.** 1,829,537 _____

    3. 2,075,821 _____   **4.** 5,380,964 _____

B. Use <, >, or = to compare.

    1. 514 ____ 541   **2.** 499 ____ 501   **3.** 103,423 ____ 99,854

C. Round each number to the given place.

    1. Nearest ten

        a. 26 _____   **b.** 254 _____   **c.** 1,076 _____

    2. Nearest hundred

        a. 146 _____   **b.** 1,912 _____   **c.** 87,659 _____

    3. Nearest thousand

        a. 26,159 _____   **b.** 47,062 _____   **c.** 5,816 _____

    4. Nearest ten thousand

        a. 14,628 _____   **b.** 45,987 _____   **c.** 733,152 _____

CRITICAL THINKING

Use the digits 0, 1, 2, 3, 4, 5, and 6 to answer the questions.

    1. What is the greatest number you can write? _____

    2. What is the least number you can write? _____

Name _____ Date _____

 1 **Adding Whole Numbers** **Exercise 2**

Lesson 1.4

Write *true* or *false* after each sentence. If the sentence is false, change the underlined word or words to make it true.

1. When you find the sum, you use <u>subtraction</u>.

_____

2. Two numbers added together are called <u>addends</u>.

_____

3. If the total in a column <u>is five or more</u>, you need to regroup.

_____

4. To add large numbers, start with the digits <u>in the ones place</u>.

_____

CRITICAL THINKING

Solve the problems.

1. Alexia collects baseball cards. She now owns 54 cards. She plans to buy 15 more cards at a card show. How many cards will she then own?

2. A basketball team scored 42 points in the first half and 59 points in the second half. The opposing team scored 105 points in the entire game. Did the home team or the opposing team win the game?

3. A farmer planted 55 acres of wheat, 27 acres of corn, and 41 acres of barley. How many acres in all did she plant?

Name _____ Date _____

 1 ▷ **Subtracting Whole Numbers and Estimation** Exercise 3

Lessons 1.5 and 1.6

A. Circle the correct answer for each expression.

1. 23 − 10
   a. 3   **b.** 13   **c.** 33

2. 74 − 39
   a. 35   **b.** 45   **c.** 15

3. Find the difference of 505 and 179.
   a. 684   **b.** 336   **c.** 326

4. Subtract 1,298 from 2,000.
   a. 712   **b.** 702   **c.** 802

5. Subtract 241 from 1,403.
   a. 1,162   **b.** 1,262   **c.** 1,644

B. Round to the given place. Then, estimate the sum or difference.

1. Round to the nearest tens.

   a. 765 + 952 _____

   b. 63 + 27 + 45 _____

   c. 18 + 24 + 16 + 5 _____

2. Round to the nearest hundreds.

   a. 456 − 137 _____

   b. 202 − 96 _____

   c. 847 + 968 + 305 _____

3. Round to the nearest thousands.

   a. 2,532 + 1,320 _____

   b. 8,296 − 7,631 _____

   c. 5,018 + 3,487 + 8,723 _____

Name _____ Date _____

 1 ▸ **Using Exponents**   **Exercise 4**

Lessons 1.7 and 1.8

A. Find the products.

1. 28×6 _____

2. 42×5 _____

3. 37×4 _____

4.   15
    $\times\, 14$

5.   95
    $\times\, 38$

6.   86
    $\times\, 40$

7. 8^2 _____

8. 4^3 _____

9. 3^4 _____

B. Write using exponents.

1. $2 \times 2 \times 2 \times 2$ _____

2. $7 \times 7 \times 7$ _____

3. $9 \times 9 \times 4 \times 4 \times 4$ _____

4. $5 \times 5 \times 3 \times 3 \times 3 \times 3$ _____

CRITICAL THINKING

Solve the problems.

1. A music shop has a case to display compact discs. The case has 15 sections, and each section can hold 18 CDs. How many CDs can this case display?

2. An office manager ordered 12 boxes of pencils. Each box contained 10 packages of pencils. Each package contained 5 pencils. How many pencils did the office manager order?

Name _____ Date _____

 1 ▸ **Estimating Using Division and Multiplication** Exercise 5

Lessons 1.9 and 1.10

Divide.

1. 3)493

2. 5)796

3. 3)1529

4. 7)4356

5. 21)394

6. 86)423

7. 32)2,478

8. 45)7,326

9. 78)2,439

CRITICAL THINKING

Circle the correct estimate for each example on the chart.
Then, use the estimate to help you find the exact answer.

	Estimate		Exact Answer
1. 8)527	6	65	
2. 17 × 21	200	400	
3. 453 ÷ 32	1	14	
4. 64 × 29	1,800	2,100	

1 ▸ Problem Solving Activities

Exercise 6

Lessons 1.4 to 1.9 and 1.12

Add, subtract, multiply, or divide.

1. $15,462 + 7,479$ _____

2. $1,076 - 988$ _____

3. 96×42 _____

4. $7,269 \div 54$ _____

5. $3^2 \times 2^4$ _____

6. 853×24 _____

CRITICAL THINKING

Solve the problems.

1. A basketball player starts jumping rope to increase his quickness. The first day he jumps rope for five minutes. Each day he adds one minute to the time. He jumps rope for one week. How many minutes will he jump on the seventh day?

2. The temperature at 6 A.M. was 60°. By noon, the temperature had increased 15°. By 3 P.M. it had increased 10° more. At 9 P.M. the temperature dropped 5°. What was the temperature at 9 P.M.?

3. Susan bought 1 roll of 200 stamps, 3 strips of 10 stamps each, and 8 extra stamps. How many stamps did Susan purchase?

4. Renée had $300 for back-to-school items. She spent $42 on school supplies, $69 on sneakers, and $149 on clothing. About how much change did Renée have when her shopping was finished?

1 ▸ Perimeter

Exercise 7

Lesson 1.13

Find the perimeter.

1.

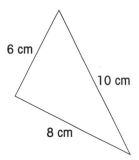

6 cm
10 cm
8 cm

2.

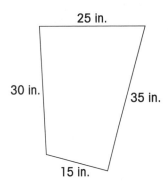

25 in.
30 in.
35 in.
15 in.

3.

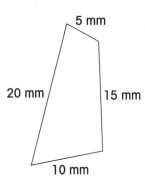

5 mm
20 mm
15 mm
10 mm

4.

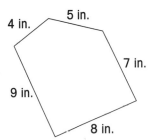

5 in.
4 in.
7 in.
9 in.
8 in.

5.

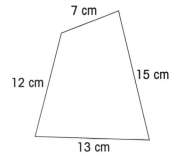

7 cm
12 cm
15 cm
13 cm

6.

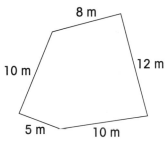

8 m
10 m
12 m
5 m
10 m

7.

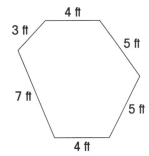

4 ft
3 ft
5 ft
7 ft
5 ft
4 ft

8.

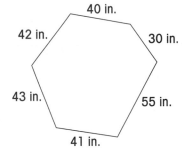

40 in.
42 in.
30 in.
43 in.
55 in.
41 in.

9.

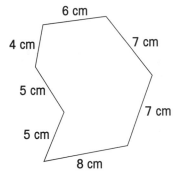

6 cm
4 cm
7 cm
5 cm
5 cm
7 cm
8 cm

CRITICAL THINKING

Find the perimeter.

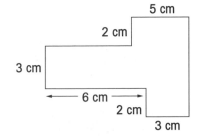

5 cm
2 cm
3 cm
6 cm
2 cm
3 cm

2 ▶ Number Expressions Using Addition and Multiplication

Exercise 8

Lessons 2.1 and 2.2

A. Write *true* or *false* after each sentence. If the sentence is false, change the underlined numbers or words to make it true.

1. To find the <u>value</u> of a number expression, do the operations.

_____

2. There are several ways to show multiplication: <u>3×2, $3(2)$, and $3 \div 2$.</u>

_____

3. A single number <u>is not</u> a number expression.

_____

B. Find the value of each number expression.

1. $4 + 25$ _____

2. $2(8)$ _____

3. $40 - 15$ _____

4. $32 + 4 - 2$ _____

5. $5 \bullet 7 - 2$ _____

6. $52 + 4 \bullet 23$ _____

CRITICAL THINKING

Solve the problems.

1. Jerome and two friends went fishing. His two friends caught 6 catfish each. Jerome caught 4 catfish. Write a number expression for the problem. How many fish did the boys catch together?

2. Carla bought two pair of shoes for $25 each. She had a $2 discount. Write a number expression for the problem. How much did Carla spend?

Name _____ Date _____

2 ▸ **Working with Expressions**   **Exercise 9**

Lesson 2.2

A. Find the value.

    1. 2(20) _____

    2. 31 + 23 _____

    3. 3 • 5 − 4 _____

    4. 24 ÷ 6 _____

    5. 15 − 12 _____

    6. 42(3) − 15 _____

B. Simplify.

    1. $2^3 - 3 \cdot 2$ _____

    2. 3 + 15 − 3 − 1 _____

    3. $4^2 \div 2^3 - 1$ _____

    4. $3 + 2^3 \cdot 3 \div 6$ _____

    5. 42 ÷ 7 • 3 _____

    6. $25 - 5^2 + 4$ _____

CRITICAL THINKING

Solve the problems.

    1. For lunch, Miriam bought two sandwiches for $2 each. She bought a juice drink for $1. She bought a fruit cup for $1. Write a number expression for the problem. How much did Miriam's lunch cost?

    2. Find out how many people were at a school assembly. Write your answers on the lines.

        a. Two principals were present. _____

        b. There were 30 times as many students as principals. _____

        c. There were 8 times as many teachers as principals. _____

        d. Total. _____

2 ▶ Simplifying Expressions with Parentheses   Exercise 10

Lessons 2.3 to 2.5

A. Simplify each expression.

   1. $2 \cdot (3 - 2)$

      a. 4   **b.** 2   **c.** 1

   2. $(5^2 \cdot 2) - 6$

      a. 13   **b.** 38   **c.** 44

   3. $3 - (21 \div 7) + 5$

      a. 4   **b.** 0   **c.** 5

   4. $(63 \div 7) - 3 \times 3 + 2$

      a. 0   **b.** 2   **c.** 20

B. Tell whether the expressions are equivalent.
   Write *yes* or *no*.

   1. $36 \div 4$ and 3×3 _____   **2.** $15 - 2$ and $28 \div 2$ _____

   3. $(4 + 2) + 1$ and $4 + (2 + 1)$ _____   **4.** 0×9 and 3^2 _____

   5. $(4 + 2)^2$ and $4^2 + 2^2$ _____   **6.** $10 - (3 - 2)$ and $(10 - 3) - 2$ _____

CRITICAL THINKING

Solve the problem.

Mrs. Keto and Mr. Baum have the same number of books in their classrooms. They each have 20 math books. They each have 22 English books. Write an expression with parentheses for the problem. Then find the total number of books.

Equations and Properties of Operations   **Exercise 11**

Lessons 2.5 to 2.7

A. Write *true* or *false* after each sentence. If the sentence is false, change the underlined words to make it true.

  1. A number equation is a statement in which two expressions <u>are not</u> equivalent.

  _____

  2. A number equation is true if the expressions on each side of the equal sign <u>have the same value</u>.

  _____

B. Name the property shown by each number equation.

  1. $4 + 3 = 3 + 4$ _____

  2. $5 + 0 = 0 + 5 = 5$ _____

  3. $(2 + 3) + 4 = 2 + (3 + 4)$ _____

  4. $5(8) = 8(5)$ _____

  5. $6 \bullet (5 \bullet 4) = (6 \bullet 5) \bullet 4$ _____

  6. $4 \times 1 = 1 \times 4 = 4$ _____

C. Complete each equation. Name the property used.

  1. $9 + 4 = $ ____ $+ 9$ _____

  2. $5 \bullet (2 \bullet 4) = (5 \bullet 2) \bullet$ ____   _____

  3. $10 \bullet$ ____ $=$ ____ $\bullet 10 = 10$ _____

  4. $10 + $ ____ $=$ ____ $+ 10 = 10$ _____

Name _____ Date _____

Lessons 2.6 to 2.8

A. Which equation shows the property? Circle your answer.

1. Commutative Property of Addition

    a. $2 + 3 = 3 + 2$

    b. $2 \cdot 3 = 3 \cdot 2$

    c. $3 + 0 = 0 + 3 = 3$

2. Associative Property of Multiplication

    a. $2 \cdot 3 = 3 \cdot 2$

    b. $2 + (3 + 4) = (2 + 3) + 4$

    c. $2 \cdot (3 \cdot 4) = (2 \cdot 3) \cdot 4$

3. Distributive Property

    a. $2 + (3 + 4) = 2 + 3 + 4$

    b. $2(3 + 4) = 2 \cdot 3 + 2 \cdot 4$

    c. $2 + (3 \cdot 4) = 2 + (4 \cdot 3)$

4. Division Property

    a. $3 \div 3 = 1$

    b. $8 \div 2 = 4$

    c. $3 \cdot 0 = 0$

B. Use a property to complete each equation.

1. $4 \div \underline{\hspace{1cm}} = 1$

2. $0 \div 9 = \underline{\hspace{1cm}}$

3. $8 \div \underline{\hspace{1cm}} = 8$

4. $5 \cdot (4 + 7) = 5 \cdot \underline{\hspace{1cm}} + 5 \cdot 7$

5. $8 \cdot (3 - 2) = 8 \cdot \underline{\hspace{1cm}} - 8 \cdot 2$

CRITICAL THINKING

Find the value in two different ways.

$$5 \cdot (3 + 4) = 5 \cdot \underline{\hspace{1cm}} + 5 \cdot \underline{\hspace{1cm}} = \underline{\hspace{1cm}} + \underline{\hspace{1cm}} = \underline{\hspace{1cm}}$$

$$5 \cdot (3 + 4) = 5 \cdot \underline{\hspace{1cm}} = \underline{\hspace{1cm}}$$

Name _____ Date _____

 2 **Choosing the Operation** **Exercise 13**

Lesson 2.10

Give the operation.

   1. Separate into equal amounts. _____

   2. Find twice as much. _____

   3. Find the difference of two numbers. _____

   4. Find how much is left. _____

   5. Find the total. _____

CRITICAL THINKING

Write a number equation for each problem.

   1. The Pep Club sold 400 programs at the football game. There were 440 programs printed. There were 40 programs left.

   2. There were 4 buses. There were 36 people on each bus. There were 144 people traveling in all.

   3. The community gym has 30 small lockers. It has 64 big lockers. The total number of lockers is 94.

   4. Fifteen hot air balloons entered a contest. There were three balloons in each group. The balloons were separated into five groups.

Name _____ Date _____

Lesson 2.11

Find the area.

1.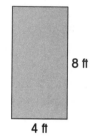

8 ft

4 ft

2.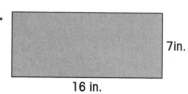

7in.

16 in.

3.

18 ft

37 ft

4.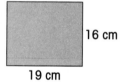

16 cm

19 cm

5.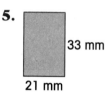

33 mm

21 mm

6.

22 yd

23 yd

CRITICAL THINKING

Find the side.

A = 4095 cm² | 91 cm

Name _____ Date _____

 3 ▸ **Defining Variable Expressions**   **Exercise 15**

Lessons 3.1 and 3.2

A. Write *true* or *false* after each sentence. If the sentence is
false, change the underlined word or words to make it true.

    1. A <u>term</u> is a letter that represents a number.

    _____

    2. A <u>variable expression</u> contains operations, numbers, and variables.

    _____

    3. In the expression $x + 4$, x and 4 are both <u>variables</u>.

    _____

    4. The expression xyz means <u>x times y times z</u>.

    _____

B. Write *like terms* or *unlike terms* next to each expression.

    1. $3xy + 5xy$ _____

    2. $21a^2 + 3a - 2$ _____

    3. $4bc - 3 + 3b$ _____

    4. $6ab - 2ab + 3ab$ _____

    5. $2 + 4xy$ _____

    6. $45rst + 45rs$ _____

CRITICAL THINKING

Read the sentence. Then write an algebraic expression for
the words.

    1. The volume of a box is length times width times height. _____

    2. Nine boys each have x dollars. _____

    3. Two boys spent x dollars and 4 girls spent y dollars. _____

    4. There are t books to divide among 7 students. _____

3 ▸ **Variable Expressions** **Exercise 16**

Lessons 3.1 to 3.5, 3.8, and 3.9

A. Match each expression with its description. Write the correct letter on the line.

_____	**1.** three terms	**a.**	$2xy - y$
_____	**2.** constant	**b.**	$2x + 3x$
_____	**3.** variable	**c.**	10
_____	**4.** two like terms	**d.**	$2xy + 3xy - xy$
_____	**5.** two unlike terms	**e.**	x

B. Evaluate each variable expression. Fill in the chart.

Expressions	Value of x	Substitution	Value of Expression
1. $x - 6$	10	$10 - 6$	
2. x^2	4		
3. $3x - 2$	4		
4. x^3	4		
5. $x \div 6$	42		

CRITICAL THINKING

Solve the problems.

1. The area of a square is side times side. The side of a square is 6 inches. Find the area.

2. The volume of a cube is side times side times side. The side is 8 feet. Find the volume.

Name _____ Date _____

3 ▸ **Using More Operations**   **Exercise 17**

Lessons 3.5 and 3.8

Write *true* or *false* on the line.

1. For $d = 2$
$3d + 5 = 11$ _____

2. For $r = 1$
$3 + 2r - 4r^2 = 9$ _____

3. For $x = 3$
$x^3 - 2 = 7$ _____

4. For $c = 5$
$2(c + 3) = 16$ _____

5. For $a = 2$
$a^3 + a^2 + 1 = 13$ _____

6. For $a = 2$ and $b = 3$
$2(b^2 - a) = 8$ _____

CRITICAL THINKING

Solve the problems.

1. To find the perimeter of a rectangle, you can use the expression $2l + 2w$ when l = length and w = width. You can also use the expression $2(l + w)$.

   a. Let $l = 7$ and $w = 5$. Find the perimeter using both expressions.

   b. Name the property that the two expressions show.

2. To find the area of a rectangle, you multiply the length and the width.

   a. The length of a rectangle is two more than the width. Write an expression for the length.

   b. If the width of this rectangle is 6, find the length.

   c. Find the area of this rectangle.

3 ▶ Simplifying Variable Expressions   Exercise 18

Lessons 3.3 to 3.6

A. Simplify by combining like terms.

1. $2x + 3x + 4$ _____

2. $a + 5a + a^2$ _____

3. $4 + 3y + y$ _____

4. $a^2 + 3a^2 - 10$ _____

5. $12 + 4b + 4 - b$ _____

6. $9 + 8n - 4 + 3n$ _____

B. Evaluate each variable expression.

1. $a + 4a - 2a$ when $a = 6$

2. $b + 5b + 10$ when $b = 2$

3. $a^2 + 2a^2 + 1$ when $a = 4$

4. $a + 2b - a - 2b$ when $a = 2$ and $b = 3$

5. $10 - 2x + 3x - 1 + x$ when $x = 3$

6. $8st + 3 - 2st$ when $s = 0$ and $t = 2$

3 ▶ Using More Variables
Exercise 19

Lessons 3.6 and 3.7

A. Evaluate each variable expression.

1. $2x + 3y$ when $x = 5$ and $y = 4$

2. $(a + 2b) \div 3$ when $a = 15$ and $b = 3$

3. lwh when $l = 4$, $w = 3$, and $h = 4$

4. $4(2a + b)$ when $a = 4$ and $b = 3$

5. $d + 3c + f$ when $d = 3$, $c = 2$, and $f = 8$

6. $x^2 - 2xy$ when $x = 5$ and $y = 2$

B. Use your calculator to evaluate the expressions.

1. $150a + 25b$ when $a = 15$ and $b = 20$

2. $a^2 - 4a + 16$ when $a = 23$

3. $600 - 2b + b^2$ when $b = 18$

4. $196 - 2x - y$ when $x = 51$ and $y = 27$

3 ▶ Using Variable Expressions

Lessons 3.6 and 3.8

Evaluate each expression.

1. $3x + 2y$ when $x = 2$ and $y = 3$

2. $a^2 - a$ when $a = 5$

3. $b^2 + 2b$ when $b = 4$

4. $a + 2b + c$ when $a = 1$, $b = 2$, and $c = 3$

5. $2s + t$ when $s = 10$ and $t = 30$

6. $5m - n^2$ when $m = 15$ and $n = 6$

CRITICAL THINKING

Solve the problems.

Harlan painted a watercolor. The length of the painting is 24 inches and the width is 18 inches. He made a frame for his painting. The framed painting is 4 inches wider and 4 inches longer than the painting.

1. What is the perimeter of Harlan's framed painting?

2. Harlan will hang the painting on a wall that measures 15 feet by 9 feet. What is the area of this wall in square inches? (Remember: 1 foot = 12 inches.)

3. Find the area of Harlan's framed painting.

4. How much wall space will be left after Harlan hangs his painting?

Name _____ Date _____

 3 ▶ **Decorating a Family Room**   **Exercise 21**

Lessons 3.8 and 3.9

CRITICAL THINKING

Help the Harrisons decorate their family room.

1. The room is 30 feet long, 24 feet wide, and 9 feet high. Find the area and the volume of the room.

2. How much carpeting in square yards would you order for this room? (Remember: 3 feet = 1 yard and 9 ft² = 1 yd².)

3. Carpeting costs $18 per square yard. How much will it cost to carpet the room?

4. The Harrisons want to wallpaper two facing walls. Each wall measures 24 feet by 9 feet. The wallpaper they chose costs $5 a square foot. How much will the wallpaper cost?

5. A wall unit for a TV, stereo system, and storage shelves is 18 feet long, 1 foot wide, and 8 feet high. What is the volume of this wall unit?

6. How much of the volume of the room will the wall unit take up?

4 ▶ Working with Variable Equations   Exercise 22

Lessons 4.1, 4.2, and 4.9

A. Is the number given a solution for the equation? Write *yes* or *no*.

1. 3; $2x + 3 = 9$ _____

2. 1; $5 - 2t = 2$ _____

3. 4; $x^2 + 5 = 13$ _____

4. 8; $x^3 - 1 = 7$ _____

5. 2; $10 - 3y = 6$ _____

6. 4; $24 \div 2n = 3$ _____

B. Tell which equations are equivalent. Write *yes* or *no*.

1. $x = 5$ and $2x + 2 = 12$ _____

2. $y = 2$ and $2y = 1$ _____

3. $a + 4 = 6$ and $a = 2$ _____

4. $y \div 4 = 8$ and $y = 8$ _____

5. $8 = 2(x + 3)$ and $x = 1$ _____

6. $28 = 4y - 8$ and $y = 9$ _____

C. Find the value of *x*.

1. $4(x + 1) = 12$

$4x + 4 = 12$

$4x +$ _____ $-$ _____ $= 12 - 4$

$4x =$ _____

$x =$ _____

Solution: _____

2. $2x + 1 = 11$

$2x + 1 -$ _____ $= 11 -$ _____

$2x =$ _____

$x =$ _____

Solution: _____

Name _____ Date _____

4 ▶ Solving Equations Using Addition or Subtraction

Exercise 23

Lessons 4.3 to 4.6

A. Write *true* or *false* after each sentence. If the sentence is false, change the underlined word or words to make it true.

1. <u>Addition</u> is the inverse of subtraction since addition "undoes" subtraction and subtraction "undoes" addition.

_____

2. Inverse operations are operations that <u>undo each other</u>.

_____

3. Division is the inverse operation of <u>subtraction</u>.

_____

4. To undo multiplication, use <u>addition</u>.

_____

B. Solve using the inverse operation. Then check the solution.

1. $x + 2 = 8$ **2.** $y + 8 = 10$

3. $15 = t - 3$ **4.** $20 = w - 3$

5. $4 + s = 13$ **6.** $16 = t + 4$

4 ▶ **Solving Equations Using Multiplication or Division** | Exercise 24

Lessons 4.7 and 4.8

Solve using inverses. Then check the solutions.

    1. $3 = x \div 15$ **2.** $0 = a \div 5$

    3. $4x = 24$ **4.** $y \div 2 = 11$

    5. $48 = 6x$ **6.** $2b = 0$

    7. $8 = x \div 7$ **8.** $5c = 60$

CRITICAL THINKING

Solve the problems.

    1. Ricco bought bagels for 6 people. He bought enough for everyone to have two bagels. How many bagels did he buy?

    2. At Funland, all rides cost $1. Angela has $21.50. How many rides can she take?

    3. The basketball team scored 52 points in the first half. The final score was 106. How many points did the team score in the second half?

Name _____ Date _____

 4 ▶ **Using More Than One Operation**   **Exercise 25**

Lesson 4.9

A. Circle the first step used to solve each equation.

1. $2x + 3 = 9$

  a. Divide by 2.   **b.** Subtract 3.   **c.** Add 3.

2. $10 = 3x - 5$

  a. Add 5.   **b.** Divide by 3.   **c.** Multiply by 5.

3. $4x - 6 = 30$

  a. Add 6.   **b.** Divide by 4.   **c.** Subtract 30.

4. $75 = 2x + 3$

  a. Subtract 3.   **b.** Multiply by 2.   **c.** Divide by 2.

5. $y \div 2 + 10 = 31$

  a. Add 10.   **b.** Subtract 10.   **c.** Divide by 2.

B. Use the solutions to complete the puzzle.

1	2		3	4
5		6		
	7			8
9			10	
11		12		

ACROSS:

1. $2x + 5 = 47$

3. $x \div 4 + 2 = 12$

5. $3x + 2 = 23$

6. $4x - 10 = 90$

7. $2x + 1 = 29$

8. $5x - 6 = 4$

9. $x - 12 = 24$

10. $x + 20 = 77$

11. $x \div 5 + 2 = 3$

12. $3x - 10 = 53$

DOWN:

1. $2x - 6 = 48$

2. $5x + 1 = 6$

3. $x \div 5 + 2 = 11$

4. $2x = 0$

6. $3x - 1 = 71$

7. $x \div 2 + 1 = 9$

8. $2x - 5 = 49$

9. $2x + 3 = 73$

10. $2x - 30 = 72$

4 ▶ **Finding and Extending Patterns**   **Exercise 26**

Lesson 4.11

Find the pattern. Fill in the missing numbers.

1. 4, 8, 12, 16, 20, _____, _____, _____

2. 3, 8, 13, 18, 23, _____, _____, _____

3. 3, 6, 12, 24, 48, _____, _____, _____

4. 120, 105, 90, 75, 60, _____, _____, _____

5. 9, 18, 27, 36, 45, _____, _____, _____

6. 25, 50, 75, 100, 125, _____, _____, _____

7. 84, 77, 70, 63, 56, 49, _____, _____, _____, _____, _____, _____

8. 1, 9, 17, 25, 33, 41, 49, _____, _____, _____, _____, _____, _____

Name _____ Date _____

4 **Solving Using Formulas**   **Exercise 27**

Lesson 4.12

Use the information to find the missing value.

1. Find the length of a rectangle. The perimeter is 20 cm.
The width is 2 cm. Use $P = 2l + 2w$.

2. Find the length of the side of a triangle. Side $a = 4$ cm,
and side $b = 9$ cm. The perimeter is 19 cm. Use
$P = a + b + c$.

CRITICAL THINKING

Solve the problems.

1. A rectangular garden has an area of 32 square feet.
The length is 8 feet. Find the width.

2. A store window has a perimeter of 18 feet. The width
is 6 feet. Find the length and the area.

3. A cube is a rectangular prism. All the sides are equal. If the
volume of a cube is 27cm^3, what is the length of a side?

Name _____ Date _____

Complete the table. Use a calculator to help you.

Length	Width	Height	Volume
2	2	2	
4		4	64
8	8		512
	16	16	4,096
32	32	32	
64		64	262,144

CRITICAL THINKING

Discuss your completed table with a partner. Then write
about the pattern you see on the lines below.

_____

_____

_____

_____

_____

_____

_____

Name _____ Date _____

Lessons 5.1 and 5.2

A. Write each decimal in words. Use the word *and* for the decimal point.

1. 2.16 _____

2. 50.2 _____

3. 0.126 _____

4. 3.08 _____

5. 1.57 _____

B. Write the words as decimals.

1. Twenty and twelve hundredths _____

2. Five and three tenths _____

3. Forty-three and forty-three thousandths _____

4. Nine and fifteen thousandths _____

5. Two hundredths _____

C. Compare. Use >, <, or =.

1. 1.12 _____ 1.1   2. 46.24 _____ 46.240

3. 291.46 _____ 292.45   4. 92.016 _____ 92.03

5. .010 _____ .009   6. 124.17 _____ 124.170

D. Round each decimal to the given place.

1. Nearest tenth   2. Nearest hundredth

    a. 4.136 _____   a. 90.156 _____

    b. 21.07 _____   b. 15.997 _____

5 ▶ Adding and Subtracting Using Decimals   Exercise 30

Lesson 5.3

A. Write *true* or *false* after each sentence. If the sentence is false, change the underlined word or words to make it true.

1. To add decimals, line up the <u>decimal points</u>.

   _____

2. When adding decimals with different numbers of digits, line up the <u>numbers</u>.

   _____

3. When subtracting decimals, line up the decimal points and fill in the missing place values with <u>zeros</u>.

   _____

B. Add or subtract.

1. $4.21 + 3.15$ 2. $9.16 + 8.95$ 3. $5.01 - 3.8$

4. $8 - .01$ 5. $1.16 + 15$ 6. $1.4 + .6$

CRITICAL THINKING

Solve the problems.

1. Matthew hiked 2.3 miles in 0.6 hour. He rested. Then he hiked 3.5 miles in 0.8 hour. How far did he hike? How long did it take?

2. Lunch cost $12.54. Alexia paid with a $20 bill. How much change did she get back?

5 ▶ Multiplying and Dividing Using Decimals   Exercise 31

Lessons 5.4 and 5.6

A. Write *true* or *false* after each sentence. If the sentence is
false, change the underlined word or words to make it true.

1. When multiplying with decimals, line up the decimal <u>points</u>.

    _____

2. If you must add zeros to the product before placing a decimal point, put the
    zeros to the <u>left of the number</u>.

    _____

3. Sometimes, you must add zeros to the <u>divisor</u> before you can divide.

    _____

B. Multiply or divide.

1. 2.6×5 2. 5.1×2.14 3. $.24 \div .6$

4. $4.112 \div .40$ 5. $2.05 \times .16$ 6. $24.8 \div .08$

CRITICAL THINKING

Solve the problems.

1. Sound is used to measure ocean depth. In one second,
    a sound will travel 1.5 km through the water. It takes
    4 seconds for sound to reach the bottom. How deep is
    the ocean at this point?

2. John can work one problem in .56 minute. He works
    3.36 minutes. How many problems does he work?

5 **Using Scientific Notation**   **Exercise 32**

Lessons 5.5, 5.7, and 5.8

A. Multiply by moving the decimal point.

    1. 2.46×100 _____

    2. 0.016×10 _____

    3. 100.14×10 _____

    4. $3.16 \times 1,000$ _____

B. Divide by moving the decimal point.

    1. $1.26 \div 10$ _____

    2. $26.24 \div 100$ _____

    3. $106.5 \div 1,000$ _____

    4. $0.0014 \div 10$ _____

C. Write each number in scientific notation.

    1. $356,000$ _____

    2. $8,848$ _____

    3. $148,300,000$ _____

D. Find the number named by each.

    1. 3.49×10^2 _____

    2. 1.6×10^6 _____

    3. 4.985×10^4 _____

5 ▸ Working with Decimal Expressions   Exercise 33

Lessons 5.9 and 5.10

A. Write *true* or *false* after each sentence. If the sentence is false, change the underlined word or words to make it true.

1. You can combine <u>unlike</u> terms with decimal coefficients into one term.

_____

2. When combining like terms, you <u>must keep</u> the order of the terms with decimal coefficients.

_____

3. You can find the value of a variable expression with decimals using the rules of <u>whole numbers</u>.

_____

B. Simplify.

1. $1.4x - 3.2 + .7x$

2. $24.2a + .5 + .21a$

3. $b^2 - 2.5b + 1.5b^2$

4. $3.4ab + .2a + 4.15b$

5. $0.14y - 1.6 + 3.12y + 3.6$

6. $21.4a^2 + 3.4a - .06a^2$

C. Evaluate each variable expression.

1. $3.6y$ when $y = 1.5$

2. $2.1a + 6.3b$ when $a = .6$ and $b = .3$

3. $x^2 + y$ when $x = .24$ and $y = 3.16$

4. $5.2x + 3.1$ when $x = .06$

5 ▶ Problem Solving Using Decimals and Algebra

Lessons 5.3, 5.4, 5.6, 5.10, 5.11, and 5.13

A. Perform the operation.

    1. 1.46×2.3

    2. $2.06 + 31.2$

    3. $49.146 - 24.98$

    4. $2.3\overline{)117.99}$

B. Evaluate.

    1. $2.1x + 1.5x$ when $x = 2.1$

    2. $1.52a - .03a - 5$ when $a = 10$

C. Solve. Then check.

    1. $x - 4.7 = 1.3$

    2. $4.72 = y + 3.4$

    3. $4.7w = 34.31$

    4. $\dfrac{x}{.9} = 8.1$

    5. $8y + 7.2 = 58.4$

    6. $\dfrac{m}{5} - 3.4 = 1.1$

CRITICAL THINKING

Solve the problems.

    1. A fish under water looks 1.25 times larger than it is. A diver under water spots a shark. The shark is 4.2 feet long. How long does it look to the diver?

    2. Gene and Joan have 10 meters of fabric. They are going to make stuffed pillows. The bear pillow takes 0.8 meters of fabric. The lion pillow takes 0.6 meters of fabric. They plan to make 8 lion pillows. How many bear pillows can they make?

Name _____ Date _____

Work with a partner. Choose three popular music groups. Ask your classmates which group they like best. Complete the frequency table. Show how many like each group best.

Music Group	Tally	Frequency

CRITICAL THINKING

Write four questions about your table. Ask some classmates to answer the questions.

1. _____

_____

2. _____

_____

3. _____

_____

4. _____

_____

Name _____ Date _____

 6 ▶ **Looking at Divisibility**   **Exercise 36**

Lesson 6.1

Write *true* or *false*.

1. 12 is a factor of 48. _____ **2.** 80 is divisible by 2. _____

3. 9 is a factor of 135. _____ **4.** 91 is divisible by 13. _____

5. 137 is divisible by 4. _____ **6.** 12 is a factor of 744. _____

CRITICAL THINKING

Complete each sentence.

1. Seven is a factor of 147 because _____

_____

2. Seven is not a factor of 243 because _____

_____

3. Could a number have a factor greater than the number itself? Explain.

_____

_____

4. All even numbers are divisible by 2 because _____

_____

Name _____ Date _____

 6 ▶ **Working with Factors and Multiples**   **Exercise 37**

Lesson 6.2

A. Circle the correct answer.

   1. The factors of 21 are

      a. 3 and 7   **b.** 1, 3, 7, 21, 42   **c.** 1, 3, 7, 21

   2. The greatest common factor of 48 and 32 is

      a. 9   **b.** 16   **c.** 48

   3. The greatest common factor of 1 and any number is

      a. 1   **b.** that number   **c.** a multiple of the number

B. Find the factors of each number.

   1. 18 _____

   2. 27 _____

   3. 64 _____

   4. 33 _____

   5. 102 _____

   6. 72 _____

C. Find the greatest common factor for each pair of numbers.
   Use the answers from Section B above.

   1. 18 and 72 _____   **2.** 33 and 27 _____   **3.** 64 and 102 _____

6 ▷ Prime and Composite Numbers

Lesson 6.3

Exercise 38

A. Write the first nine multiples of each number.

1. 2 _____

2. 3 _____

3. 4 _____

4. 5 _____

5. 7 _____

6. 9 _____

B. What is the difference between a common multiple and the least common multiple?

_____

_____

C. Find the least common multiple for each pair of numbers. Use the answers from Section A above.

1. 2 and 7 _____   **2.** 3 and 7 _____

3. 2 and 4 _____   **4.** 4 and 5 _____

CRITICAL THINKING

Follow the steps to find a pattern for multiples of nine.

1. List the first 10 multiples of nine. _____

2. For each multiple, find the sum of the ones digit and the tens digit. _____

_____

3. Describe the pattern. _____

Name _____ Date _____

 6 ► **Factoring Using Prime Numbers**   **Exercise 39**

Lesson 6.4

CRITICAL THINKING

Use the Sieve of Eratosthenes.
Find all the prime numbers from
1 to 100. Follow the directions below.

Hundreds Chart

1	2	3	4	5	6	7	8	9	10
11	12	13	14	15	16	17	18	19	20
21	22	23	24	25	26	27	28	29	30
31	32	33	34	35	36	37	38	39	40
41	42	43	44	45	46	47	48	49	50
51	52	53	54	55	56	57	58	59	60
61	62	63	64	65	66	67	68	69	70
71	72	73	74	75	76	77	78	79	80
81	82	83	84	85	86	87	88	89	90
91	92	93	94	95	96	97	98	99	100

1. Cross out 1 since it is neither prime nor composite.

2. Circle 2, the first prime number. Two is the only even prime number. Now cross out all multiples of 2, such as 4, 6, 8, 10, and so on, to 100. All these numbers are composite since 2 is a factor of the numbers.

3. Circle 3, the next prime number. Now cross out all multiples of 3 that are not even, such as 9, 15, and so on. All these numbers are composite since 3 is a factor of each one.

4. Circle 5, the next prime number. Cross out all multiples of 5, such as 10, 15, 20, 25, and so on. Some of these numbers may already be crossed out.

5. Circle 7, the next prime number. Cross out all multiples of 7, such as 14, 21, 28, and so on. Some of these numbers may already be crossed out.

6. Look at the chart. Are the remaining numbers all prime? How do you know?

   _____

7. List all the prime numbers from 1 to 100 from the chart. _____

   _____

6 ▶ Prime Factorization

Exercise 40

Lesson 6.5

Find the prime factorization. Write your answer using exponents whenever possible.

1. 56 _____

2. 120 _____

3. 24 _____

4. 39 _____

5. 76 _____

6. 99 _____

CRITICAL THINKING

Write the answers.

1. Explain how you found the prime factorization of 99 in number 6 of the section above.

_____

_____

_____

2. Can you have more than one prime factorization of any composite number? Explain. (The order of the factors does not matter.)

_____

_____

_____

6 ▶ Problem Solving Using Factors and Multiples

Exercise 41

Lesson 6.7

CRITICAL THINKING

Solve the problems.

1. Annie wants to build an outdoor deck in her back yard in the shape of a rectangle. She wants the area to be 30 ft^2. How many different lengths and widths can the deck have? Use whole numbers.

	(a)	**(b)**	**(c)**	**(d)**
Length				
Width				

2. The dot patterns below are called triangular numbers. They are called triangular numbers because they make triangles. What would the next triangular number be? Draw the dot pattern.

     1   3   6   10

3. These dot patterns show square numbers. Find the next square number.

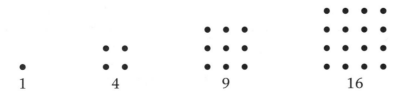

     1   4   9   16

Name _____ Date _____

Look at the bar graph. It shows information about new car sales.

Talk about the graph with a group. Then, together, write at least four questions based on the graph. Ask another group to answer your questions.

1. _____

_____

2. _____

_____

3. _____

_____

4. _____

_____

7 ⟩ **What Is a Fraction?** Exercise 43

Lesson 7.1

A. Complete the table.

Numerator	3	2	5	4		5	
Denominator	7	5	11				8
Fraction	$\frac{3}{7}$			$\frac{4}{9}$	$\frac{11}{21}$	$\frac{5}{2}$	$\frac{1}{8}$

B. Shade to show the given fraction.

1. $\frac{5}{6}$

2. $\frac{4}{9}$

3. $\frac{5}{5}$

4. $\frac{1}{3}$

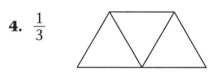

CRITICAL THINKING

Solve the problems.

1. There are 52 cars in a lot. Nine of the cars are red. What fraction shows how many of the cars are red?

2. Scott and Carla are shooting free throws. Scott makes 13. Carla makes 17. They each shoot 20 free throws. What fraction of shots does each make?

7 ▶ **Working with Fractions and Mixed Numbers**

Exercise 44

Lessons 7.2 and 7.3

A. Write *true* or *false* after each sentence. If the sentence is false, change the underlined word or words to make it true.

1. When the numerator is larger than the denominator, it is called an <u>improper</u> fraction.

   _____

2. The <u>numerator</u> is the bottom number in the fraction.

   _____

3. A mixed number <u>does not</u> contain a fraction.

   _____

B. Write a mixed number for each problem.

1. Eight and seven twelfths _____   2. Five and three tenths _____

3. Write the mixed number for the shaded area.

a. _____

b. _____

C. Write a whole number or mixed number for each.

1. $\dfrac{9}{3}$ 2. $\dfrac{7}{2}$ 3. $\dfrac{6}{6}$ 4. $\dfrac{24}{5}$

D. Write an improper fraction for each.

1. $3\dfrac{2}{7}$ 2. $5\dfrac{1}{5}$ 3. $7\dfrac{2}{3}$ 4. $6\dfrac{1}{8}$

7 Finding Equivalent Fractions   Exercise 45

Lessons 7.4 to 7.6

Write equivalent fractions.

1. Multiply the numerator and the denominator by 3.

   a. $\frac{2}{5}$ **b.** $\frac{5}{6}$ **c.** $\frac{7}{8}$

2. Multiply the numerator and the denominator by 4 and then by 5.

   a. $\frac{3}{4}$ **b.** $\frac{7}{10}$ **c.** $\frac{5}{9}$

3. For each fraction, find two equivalent fractions.

   a. $\frac{3}{8}$ **b.** $\frac{5}{7}$

   c. $\frac{8}{9}$ **d.** $\frac{3}{10}$

CRITICAL THINKING

Complete the table.

Numerator	4	2	3	7			
Denominator	8	10	9	28			24
Fraction	$\frac{4}{8}$	$\frac{2}{10}$			$\frac{15}{18}$	$\frac{12}{16}$	
Fraction in Lowest Terms	$\frac{1}{2}$					$\frac{3}{4}$	$\frac{1}{8}$

7 ▶ **Comparing Fractions**   **Exercise 46**

Lessons 7.6 and 7.7

A. Write *true* or *false* after each sentence. If the sentence is false, change the underlined word or words to make it true.

1. Fractions with different denominators are called <u>unlike</u> fractions.

_____

2. Like fractions have the same <u>amount</u>.

_____

3. If the greatest common factor of the numerator and denominator is 1, the fraction is <u>in lowest terms</u>.

_____

B. Use >, <, or = to compare.

1. $\frac{5}{8}$ _____ $\frac{3}{5}$ **2.** $\frac{5}{8}$ _____ $\frac{8}{11}$ **3.** $\frac{7}{15}$ _____ $\frac{3}{7}$

4. $\frac{4}{5}$ _____ $\frac{8}{10}$ **5.** $\frac{3}{2}$ _____ $\frac{7}{4}$ **6.** $\frac{5}{3}$ _____ $\frac{12}{7}$

CRITICAL THINKING

Solve the problems.

1. Belinda spent $\frac{9}{10}$ hour at the gym. Paco spent $\frac{4}{5}$ hour at the gym. Who spent more time at the gym?

2. Antonio jogged $\frac{7}{8}$ mile. Marty jogged $\frac{5}{6}$ mile. Who jogged a greater distance?

Name _____ Date _____

 7 ▶ **Writing Fractions and Decimals** **Exercise 47**

Lesson 7.8

A. Write a fraction to represent the pictures. Reduce each fraction.

1.

_____

2.

_____

3.

_____

B. Write each decimal as a fraction in lowest terms.

1. 0.4 _____   **2.** 0.25 _____

3. 0.2 _____   **4.** 0.5 _____

5. 0.125 _____   **6.** 3.7 _____

CRITICAL THINKING

Solve the problems.

1. John Stockton's free-throw average during the NBA playoffs is .87. Write this as a fraction.

2. School meets 180 days per year. There are 365 days in a non-leap year.

    a. Write a fraction for the number of school days. _____

    b. Write the fraction as a decimal. Round to the nearest

      hundredths. _____

Name _____ Date _____

 7 ▶ **Counting and Using Fractions** **Exercise 48**

Lessons 7.3 and 7.10

CRITICAL THINKING

Solve the problems.

1. For lunch, you have a choice of 3 soups, 4 sandwiches, and 2 kinds of fruit. How many choices do you have?

2. Sandy has 4 pairs of shorts, 6 polo shirts, and 3 caps. How many outfits can Sandy put together?

3. Below is the recipe for fruit punch. Write each amount as a mixed number or a whole number.

   $\frac{15}{3}$ cups lemon juice   _____

   $\frac{21}{4}$ cups grape juice   _____

   $\frac{42}{4}$ cups orange juice   _____

   $\frac{38}{6}$ cups apple juice   _____

   $\frac{13}{3}$ cups pineapple juice   _____

4. Robyn shared $2\frac{1}{8}$ oranges with her friends. Each friend received $\frac{1}{8}$ of an

   orange. How many friends does Robyn have? _____

5. Austin, Dee, and Sandra just had lunch. The total bill is $15.30. How much should each person pay if they divide the bill evenly? Write this amount as a mixed number.

   _____

7 ▶ **Finding Averages** **Exercise 49**

Lesson 7.11

Ask five people the following questions. Record their answers. Then find the averages. Use the table below.

1. How many hours do you sleep each night?

2. How many minutes do you talk on the telephone each day?

3. How many hours a week do you watch television?

	Question 1	Question 2	Question 3
1.			
2.			
3.			
4.			
5.			
Sum:		Sum:	Sum:
Average:		Average:	Average:

CRITICAL THINKING

Add your own answer to each question. Find the new averages. Ask a partner to check your work.

1. _____

New average: _____

2. _____

New average: _____

3. _____

New average: _____

8 ▶ Fractions with Like Denominators   Exercise 50

Lesson 8.1

Circle the correct answer for each example.

1. $\dfrac{2}{7} + \dfrac{3}{7}$

   a. $\dfrac{5}{14}$ **b.** $\dfrac{5}{7}$ **c.** $\dfrac{6}{7}$

2. $\dfrac{8}{9} - \dfrac{5}{9}$

   a. $\dfrac{4}{18}$ **b.** $\dfrac{13}{9}$ **c.** $\dfrac{3}{9}$

3. $\dfrac{4}{11} + \dfrac{7}{11}$

   a. 1   **b.** $\dfrac{11}{12}$ **c.** $\dfrac{1}{2}$

4. $\dfrac{8}{3} - \dfrac{2}{3}$

   a. 2   **b.** 1   **c.** $\dfrac{5}{3}$

CRITICAL THINKING

Solve the problems.

1. Marcus mows $\frac{7}{15}$ of the lawn. Glen mows $\frac{8}{15}$ of the lawn. How much did they mow together?

2. Jorge lifts weights for $1\frac{1}{4}$ hours. He runs $\frac{3}{4}$ hour. How long does he work out?

3. Yoshi rode his bike $\frac{7}{4}$ miles. He then walked $\frac{3}{4}$ mile. How much farther did he bike than walk?

4. April practices basketball during the week. She practices $\frac{3}{2}$ hours on Monday. She practices $\frac{5}{2}$ hours on Thursday.

   a. How long does she practice in one week?

   b. Which day did she practice longer? How much longer?

8 ▶ **Fractions with Unlike Denominators**   **Exercise 51**

Lesson 8.2 to 8.4

Follow the steps. Then add.

1. $\frac{2}{5} + \frac{3}{10} =$ Think: $\frac{2}{5} = \frac{2 \times 2}{5 \times 2} = \frac{4}{10} \rightarrow \frac{4}{10} + \frac{3}{10} = \frac{7}{10}$

2. $\frac{1}{3} + \frac{5}{6} =$ Think: $\frac{1}{3} = \frac{1 \times 2}{3 \times 2} = \frac{}{6} \rightarrow \frac{}{6} + \frac{5}{6} = \frac{}{6}$

3. $\frac{5}{12} - \frac{1}{4} =$ Think: $\frac{1}{4} = \frac{1 \times 3}{4 \times 3} = \frac{}{12} \rightarrow \frac{5}{12} - \frac{}{12} = \frac{}{12}$

4. $\frac{3}{4} - \frac{1}{2} =$ Think: $\frac{1}{2} = \frac{1 \times 2}{2 \times 2} = \frac{}{4} \rightarrow \frac{3}{4} - \frac{}{4} = \frac{}{4}$

CRITICAL THINKING

Solve the problems.

1. Janice ran $\frac{7}{8}$ mile. She walked $\frac{3}{4}$ mile. How far did she run and walk?

2. Kim umpires baseball games for $7\frac{1}{2}$ hours. He also works at the snack concession for $\frac{3}{4}$ hour. How long does he work altogether?

3. Mrs. Gorsky bought $\frac{7}{10}$ yard of blue ribbon. She also bought $\frac{3}{5}$ yard of red ribbon. How much ribbon did she buy?

4. Abdul painted $\frac{3}{10}$ of a house in the morning. He painted $\frac{3}{5}$ of the house in the afternoon. How much of the house did he paint in one day?

8 ▶ Adding and Subtracting Mixed Numbers   Exercise 52

Lessons 8.5 and 8.6

Add or subtract.

1. $2\frac{1}{3} + 3\frac{5}{6}$

2. $7\frac{1}{3} - 2\frac{5}{6}$

3. $4\frac{3}{5} - 1\frac{1}{4}$

4. $6 + 2\frac{1}{2}$

5. $5\frac{1}{2} + 1\frac{5}{12}$

6. $4 - 1\frac{9}{10}$

7. $7\frac{1}{2} - 2\frac{1}{6}$

8. $8\frac{1}{4} + 1\frac{3}{8}$

9. $5 - 1\frac{9}{10}$

CRITICAL THINKING

Solve the problems.

1. Damon and Paul went fishing. Damon caught $4\frac{1}{2}$ pounds of fish. Paul caught $2\frac{3}{4}$ pounds of fish.

    a. How much fish did Damon and Paul catch together?

    b. How many more pounds did Damon catch than Paul?

2. Rochelle and Lucille are on the 2-mile relay team. Rochelle runs $\frac{1}{4}$ mile and Lucille runs 1 mile.

    a. How far do they run together?

    b. How far do the other team members have to run?

    c. How much farther does Lucille run than Rochelle?

8 ▸ Evaluating Variable Expressions   Exercise 53

Lessons 8.3, 8.4, and 8.7

A. Evaluate for each expression.

1. Find the value of $x - y$ when $x = 7\frac{3}{4}$ and $y = 2\frac{3}{8}$.

2. Find the value of $x + y$ when $x = 3\frac{1}{3}$ and $y = 4\frac{5}{9}$.

3. Find the value of $r + 4$ when $r = 3\frac{1}{3}$.

B. Find the perimeter of each triangle.

1.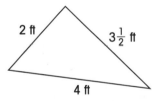

   $P =$ _____

2.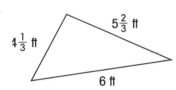

   $P =$ _____

3.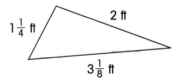

   $P =$ _____

CRITICAL THINKING

Answer the question.

Compare the perimeters of the triangles. How much greater is

the largest perimeter than the smallest? _____

Name _____ Date _____

8 ▸ Solving Two-step Equations Using Mixed Numbers

Exercise 54

Lesson 8.8

A. Solve. Then check.

1. $r - \frac{1}{2} = 2$

2. $5\frac{1}{4} = a + 1$

3. $x + \frac{2}{9} = 4\frac{5}{9}$

4. $c - 1\frac{3}{5} = \frac{9}{10}$

5. $3\frac{1}{7} = r + 2$

6. $4\frac{1}{3} = x + 3$

B. Circle the correct solution for each equation. Then check the solution.

1. $m - \frac{1}{2} = 4$, then $m =$

   a. $3\frac{1}{2}$ **b.** 2 **c.** $4\frac{1}{2}$

2. $2\frac{3}{4} = n + \frac{1}{4}$, then $n =$

   a. $2\frac{1}{2}$ **b.** 3 **c.** $2\frac{1}{4}$

3. $p + 3\frac{1}{9} = 7\frac{7}{9}$, then $p =$

   a. $4\frac{2}{3}$ **b.** $4\frac{2}{9}$ **c.** $10\frac{8}{9}$

4. $5\frac{2}{5} = h - \frac{1}{10}$, then $h =$

   a. $5\frac{5}{15}$ **b.** $5\frac{1}{2}$ **c.** $5\frac{3}{10}$

5. $\frac{1}{8} + c = \frac{9}{8}$, then $c =$

   a. $1\frac{1}{4}$ **b.** 1 **c.** $\frac{1}{2}$

8 ▷ **Problem Solving Using Mixed Numbers**   **Exercise 55**

Lesson 8.10

CRITICAL THINKING

Solve the problems if you can. Tell whether there is too much information or too little information.

1. Lexi buys a stereo. She has $75.43. The stereo costs $72. The speakers cost $20. How much money will Lexi have after she buys the stereo?

2. Devan collects stamps and coins. She has 90 flower stamps, 37 angel stamps, and 46 presidential stamps. She has 150 coins. How many stamps does she have?

3. Pablo rents surfboards for $7.00 per hour. He rented 17 surfboards. How much did he make renting surfboards?

4. Gwen has a nursery. She grows 23 different kinds of plants. It takes 5 hours to feed and water all the plants. She spends an equal amount of time on each plant. How long does she spend on each plant?

5. Raoul works 5 days a week. He works $8\frac{1}{2}$ hours a day. He plays golf on Saturday. How much does he make in one week?

Finding the Mode and Median   Exercise 56

Lesson 8.11

Work with a partner. Follow the steps.

STEP 1   Create two sets of index cards. Each set should contain the numbers 1 through 20.

STEP 2   Shuffle the 40 cards together. Pick nine cards.

STEP 3   Find the mode, if any. Then find the median.

STEP 4   Return the cards to the deck. Reshuffle. Now pick ten cards.

STEP 5   Find the mode, if any. Then find the median.

STEP 6   Play six rounds. Use the space below to record the results. (Save the cards for another game.)

    Round 1   median   _____

                   mode   _____

    Round 2   median   _____

                   mode   _____

    Round 3   median   _____

                   mode   _____

    Round 4   median   _____

                   mode   _____

    Round 5   median   _____

                   mode   _____

    Round 6   median   _____

                   mode   _____

9 ▶ Multiplying Mixed Numbers **Exercise 57**

Lessons 9.1, 9.2, and 9.4

Multiply.

1. $\dfrac{2}{5} \times \dfrac{3}{7}$ 2. $\dfrac{5}{8} \times 7$ 3. $\dfrac{1}{9} \times \dfrac{2}{9}$ 4. $1 \times \dfrac{5}{7}$

5. $\dfrac{7}{8} \times \dfrac{2}{5}$ 6. $6 \times \dfrac{1}{3}$ 7. $\dfrac{25}{26} \times \dfrac{2}{5}$ 8. $\dfrac{9}{13} \times \dfrac{1}{3}$

CRITICAL THINKING

Solve the problem.

1. Charlene works 11 weeks during the summer as a lifeguard. She works $3\frac{1}{2}$ days each week. How many days does Charlene work in 11 weeks?

2. It costs $4 to rent a canoe for half an hour.

   a. Kharry rented a canoe for $3\frac{1}{2}$ hours. How much did he pay?

   b. Cynthia and Jill rent a canoe 3 times a week. They keep the canoe for $2\frac{1}{2}$ hours each time. How much do they pay each week?

3. A room is $12\frac{1}{2}$ feet wide and $10\frac{2}{5}$ feet long. What is the area of the room? (Use $A = l \times w$)

4. Jennifer and Nathan install carpet. It takes $\frac{1}{2}$ hour to carpet one room. How long would it take to carpet 19 rooms?

5. The carpet store had a piece of carpet $7\frac{1}{4}$ feet long. Radwan bought $\frac{1}{2}$ of the piece. How long was the piece Radwan bought?

9   **Dividing Using Mixed Numbers**   **Exercise 58**

Lessons 9.3 and 9.4

Divide.

1. $\dfrac{7}{10} \div \dfrac{1}{4}$ 2. $\dfrac{13}{15} \div \dfrac{1}{3}$ 3. $\dfrac{3}{5} \div \dfrac{21}{25}$

4. $4\dfrac{1}{2} \div 2\dfrac{1}{4}$ 5. $4\dfrac{1}{7} \div 3\dfrac{1}{7}$ 6. $8\dfrac{1}{4} \div 5\dfrac{1}{2}$

7. $6\dfrac{1}{3} \div 6\dfrac{2}{9}$ 8. $12\dfrac{3}{4} \div 9\dfrac{3}{4}$ 9. $1\dfrac{3}{5} \div 7\dfrac{1}{10}$

CRITICAL THINKING

Solve the problems.

1. A piece of rope is $20\dfrac{1}{4}$ feet long. How many $2\dfrac{1}{4}$ foot long pieces can you cut?

2. A package of ground turkey weighs $3\dfrac{3}{5}$ pounds. How many $\dfrac{3}{10}$ pound patties can you make?

Simplifying Expressions with Mixed Numbers

Exercise 59

Lesson 9.5

A. Simplify.

1. $3x + \dfrac{2}{3}x$

2. $\dfrac{1}{2}y - \dfrac{1}{4}y$

3. $\dfrac{7}{12}r + \dfrac{5}{12}r$

4. $\dfrac{a}{4} + \dfrac{2}{5}a + \dfrac{1}{7}b$

5. $5y + 2x - \dfrac{y}{4}$

6. $\dfrac{h}{2} + \dfrac{h}{4} + \dfrac{3}{4}h$

B. Match each variable expression with its simplified form. Write the correct letter on the line.

_____ 1. $8c - \dfrac{2}{3}f + \dfrac{1}{2}c$

a. $\dfrac{2}{9}g + \dfrac{3}{10}r$

_____ 2. $6c - \dfrac{3}{4}c + \dfrac{1}{2}f$

b. $6x^2 + 2\dfrac{1}{3}y$

_____ 3. $\dfrac{2}{9}g + \dfrac{1}{2}r - \dfrac{1}{5}r$

c. $\dfrac{2}{3}m + 7n$

_____ 4. $\dfrac{7}{9}g - \dfrac{1}{10}r - \dfrac{5}{9}g$

d. $5\dfrac{1}{4}c + \dfrac{1}{2}f$

_____ 5. $\dfrac{4}{3}w + \dfrac{2}{3}w + \dfrac{1}{9}w$

e. $2\dfrac{1}{9}w$

_____ 6. $m + 7n - \dfrac{1}{3}m$

f. $\dfrac{2}{9}g - \dfrac{1}{10}r$

_____ 7. $2x^2 + 2\dfrac{1}{3}y + 4x^2$

g. $\dfrac{10}{13}y$

_____ 8. $\dfrac{3}{13}y + \dfrac{5}{13}y + \dfrac{2}{13}y$

h. $8\dfrac{1}{2}c - \dfrac{2}{3}f$

Evaluating Expressions with Mixed Numbers   **Exercise 60**

Lesson 9.6

Circle the correct answer.

1. The value of *lw* when *l* = 5 and *w* = $2\frac{1}{2}$ is

   a. $7\frac{1}{2}$ **b.** $12\frac{1}{2}$ **c.** $11\frac{1}{2}$

2. The value of 4*s* when *s* = $3\frac{1}{5}$ is

   a. $12\frac{4}{5}$ **b.** 64   **c.** $12\frac{1}{5}$

3. The value of *d* ÷ *r* when *d* = $2\frac{1}{3}$ and *r* = $3\frac{1}{9}$ is

   a. $6\frac{1}{3}$ **b.** $1\frac{1}{3}$ **c.** $\frac{3}{4}$

4. The value of 2*a* − 3*b* when *a* = 2 and *b* = $\frac{1}{2}$ is

   a. $3\frac{1}{2}$ **b.** $\frac{1}{2}$ **c.** $2\frac{1}{2}$

CRITICAL THINKING

Solve the problems.

1. The area of a sandbox is 36 ft square. The length is $12\frac{1}{2}$ ft. Find the width. (Use *A* = *l* × *w*.)

2. Perry receives $45 for an allowance. He spent $\frac{2}{3}$ of his allowance on shorts. How much did he have left?

3. Tickets to the opera cost $25 each. Dinner costs $10 each. Joey and Micah go to the opera and dinner. What is the total cost for both boys? What part of the total cost is the opera?

Equations with Fractions and Mixed Numbers   **Exercise 61**

Lesson 9.7

A. Solve. Then check your answer.

1. $3\frac{1}{2}x = 21$

2. $\frac{5}{3}b = 10$

3. $\frac{1}{4}a = 3$

4. $\frac{1}{5}y = 4$

5. $\frac{x}{6} + \frac{1}{3} = \frac{2}{3}$

6. $4n = 2\frac{2}{5}$

B. Circle the correct solution for each equation. Then check the solution.

1. $5m = \frac{1}{2}$

   a. 10   **b.** $\frac{1}{10}$ **c.** $9\frac{3}{4}$

2. $\frac{3}{4}d = 9$

   a. 12   **b.** $\frac{1}{12}$ **c.** $9\frac{3}{4}$

3. $\frac{1}{3}g - 2 = 1$

   a. 9   **b.** 1   **c.** $1\frac{1}{3}$

4. $7 = 3\frac{1}{2}a$

   a. $24\frac{1}{2}$ **b.** 2   **c.** $9\frac{3}{2}$

Name _____ Date _____

Lesson 9.9

A. The following table provides the price per pound for some fruits.

Fruit	Price Per Pound
Peaches	78¢
Plums	98¢
Apples	88¢
Bananas	58¢

Solve each problem by using the table.

1. What is the cost of $1\frac{1}{2}$ pounds of peaches?

2. How many pounds of bananas can be bought for $1.45?

3. What is the cost of 2 pounds of apples and $\frac{1}{2}$ pound of plums?

B. Find the perimeter and area of each. Use *P = 2l + 2w* and *A = l × w.*

1.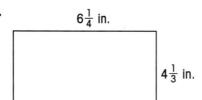
　$6\frac{1}{4}$ in.　$4\frac{1}{3}$ in.

2.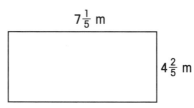
　$7\frac{1}{5}$ m　$4\frac{2}{5}$ m

3.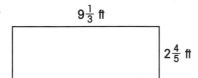
　$9\frac{5}{6}$ cm　$2\frac{1}{4}$ cm

4.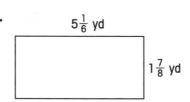
　$5\frac{1}{6}$ yd　$1\frac{7}{8}$ yd

5.
　$9\frac{1}{3}$ ft　$2\frac{4}{5}$ ft

6.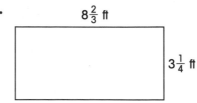
　$8\frac{2}{3}$ ft　$3\frac{1}{4}$ ft

9 **Finding Minimum, Maximum, and Range** **Exercise 63**

Lesson 9.10

Work with a partner. Follow the steps.

STEP 1 Use the deck of cards you made for Exercise 56.
Shuffle the cards.

STEP 2 Pick eight cards. Order them from smallest to largest.

STEP 3 Find the minimum, the maximum, and the range.

STEP 4 Return the cards to the deck. Reshuffle.

STEP 5 Play six rounds using different numbers
of cards. Record the results.

Round 1 minimum _____   **Round 2** minimum _____

maximum _____   maximum _____

range _____   range _____

Round 3 minimum _____   **Round 4** minimum _____

maximum _____   maximum _____

range _____   range _____

Round 5 minimum _____   **Round 6** minimum _____

maximum _____   maximum _____

range _____   range _____

10 ▶ Solving Proportions   Exercise 64

Lessons 10.1, 10.2, and 10.12

A. Write *true* or *false* after each sentence. If the sentence is
false, change the underlined word or words to make it true.

1. A ratio is a comparison of <u>two numbers</u>.

_____

2. A proportion shows that two ratios <u>are not</u> equal.

_____

3. You can find any number in a proportion as long as you know
<u>two</u> other numbers.

_____

4. You can check to see if two ratios are in the same proportion
by using the <u>cross product</u>.

_____

B. Solve the problems. Explain your work.

1. Solve: $\dfrac{4}{15} = \dfrac{x}{60}$

2. The ratio of bran muffins to packages is 8 to 1. Will
6 packages contain 50 muffins?

3. The ratio of flowers to vases is 4 to 1. There are 7 vases.
How many flowers are there?

C. Write = or ≠ for each pair of fractions.

1. $\dfrac{2}{5}$ ____ $\dfrac{8}{20}$ **2.** $\dfrac{8}{11}$ ____ $\dfrac{28}{44}$

3. $\dfrac{3}{5}$ ____ $\dfrac{24}{35}$ **4.** $\dfrac{6}{3}$ ____ $\dfrac{36}{54}$

Finding Ratios and Percents   **Exercise 65**

Lessons 10.1 and 10.3

A. Find the missing ratio or percent. Fill in the chart.

Ratio	45 to 100		9 to 100		92 to 100		
Percent		56%		89%		17%	33%

B. Write the ratio of the shaded parts to all parts.

1.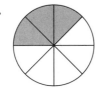

2.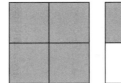

3.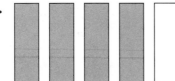

4.

C. Write a percent for the shaded part.

1.

2.

3.

4.

10 ▶ **Finding Percents and Decimals**   **Exercise 66**

Lesson 10.4

A. Circle the correct answer.

1. The decimal for 8% is

    a. 0.80   **b.** 800.0   **c.** .08

2. The percent for 1.75 is

    a. 17.5%   **b.** 175%   **c.** .0175%

3. The decimal for 37% is

    a. .37   **b.** 3.7   **c.** 37

4. The percent for .84 is

    a. 84%   **b.** .84%   **c.** 840%

B. Write a percent for each.

1. .74 = _____   **2.** 1.73 = _____   **3.** 2.95 = _____

4. .97 = _____   **5.** 3.74 = _____   **6.** .01 = _____

7. 5.07 = _____   **8.** .2 = _____   **9.** 1.14 = _____

10 Fractions and Percents

Lessons 10.5 to 10.7

Exercise 67

A. Find the missing fraction, mixed number, or percent.
   Fill in the chart.

Fraction	$\frac{1}{20}$	$\frac{1}{25}$	$\frac{3}{5}$			$\frac{3}{6}$	$\frac{19}{50}$		$\frac{125}{100}$
Percent	5%			15%	50%			75%	

B. Match each percent fact with its number equation. Write
   the correct letter on the line.

_____ **1.** 24 is 96% of 25.

_____ **2.** 40% of 145 employees is 58.

_____ **3.** 14 ft is 25% of 56 ft.

_____ **4.** 20% of 100 cars is 20 cars.

_____ **5.** 110% of 100 is 110.

_____ **6.** 45 plants is 15% of 300 plants.

_____ **7.** 12 stereos is 60% of 20 stereos.

_____ **8.** 76 bicycles is 95% of 80 bicycles.

_____ **9.** 69 is 138% of 50.

a. $14 = .25 \times 56$

b. $1.10 \times 100 = 110$

c. $76 = .95 \times 80$

d. $24 = .96 \times 25$

e. $45 = .15 \times 300$

f. $69 = 1.38 \times 50$

g. $.20 \times 100 = 20$

h. $.4 \times 145 = 58$

i. $12 = .6 \times 20$

CRITICAL THINKING

Solve the problems.

1. Nicholas bought a car for $4,800. He paid 20% in cash.
   He borrowed the rest. How much did he pay in cash?
   How much did he borrow?

2. Marjorie bought a book on sale. The sale was $\frac{1}{4}$ off.
   The original cost of the book was $20. What was the
   sale price?

10 ▶ **Solving Percent Equations**   **Exercise 68**

Lessons 10.7 to 10.9

A. Solve.

1. What number is 68% of 45?

   $.68 \times 45 = r$
   $r = ?$

2. What percent of 40 is 32?

   $P \times 40 = 32$
   $P = ?$

3. 100% of what number is 74?

   $1 \times y = 74$
   $y = ?$

B. Write an equation. Then solve the equation.

1. 75% of 25 students is about how many students?

2. What percent of 100 desks is 75?

3. 18 tables is 24% of how many tables?

4. 35% of 75 chairs is about how many chairs?

5. What percent of 86 computers is 43?

6. 20% of 30 pencils is how many pencils?

Name _____   Date _____

10 ▶ Problem Solving Using Proportions and Percents

Exercise 69

Lessons 10.8 and 10.10

CRITICAL THINKING

Solve the problems.

1. The gas tank of Amy's sports car holds 15 gallons. She used all but 6 gallons of gas. Find the % decrease of gas in her car.

2. Jessica bought a $65 sweater on sale. The sale price was $39. Find the percent decrease.

3. Andy bought a car. He paid $14,000. The dealer paid $11,000 for the car. Find the percent increase.

4. Tyler shoots 200 free throws. He makes 135 of them. What percent of free throws does he make?

5. There are 75 square feet in a roll of carpet that Jane likes. She needs 67 square feet for her house. What percent of the roll will she need?

10 ▸ Finding the Discount Price   Exercise 70

Lesson 10.13

CRITICAL THINKING

You and a partner own a discount electronics store.
You decide to have a big sale to bring in new customers.
For each item below, decide on a percent discount. Then
find the discount price.

Remember:
Original price − amount of discount = discount price

1. 26-inch television
original price: $675

2. stereo system
original price: $1,200

3. video cassette recorder
original price: $500

4. videodisc/CD player
original price: $850

5. home security system
original price: $1,500

6. deluxe camcorder
original price: $1,650

11 **Using Absolute Value and Opposites** **Exercise 71**

Lesson 11.1 and 11.2

A. Write *true* or *false* after each sentence. If the sentence is false, change the underlined number or words to make it true.

1. The integers ⁻6 and ⁻6 are opposites.

   _____

2. Absolute value means the <u>distance</u> an integer is from 0.

   _____

3. The value of $|^-1|$ is <u>1</u>.

   _____

4. Positive integers are numbers to the <u>left of</u> 0.

   _____

B. Complete the table. Give the opposite in words. Then write the opposite as an integer.

	Opposite in words	Integer
1. Gain of $5	Loss of $5	⁻5
2. Loss of $10		
3. 30°F increase in temperature		
4. 50°F decrease in temperature		
5. Loss of 12 pounds		
6. Gain of 2 pounds		

11 ▶ Adding and Subtracting Integers　　　　**Exercise 72**

Lessons 11.1 and 11.3 to 11.5

A. Tell which direction from zero you would move. Write *left* or *right*.

1. $^-6$ _____ 　　**2.** 0 _____ 　　**3.** 10 _____

4. 5 _____ 　　**5.** 2 _____ 　　**6.** $^-2$ _____

7. $^-4$ _____ 　　**8.** 6 _____ 　　**9.** $^-10$ _____

B. Add or subtract. Use a number line if you need help.

1. $^-3 + 2$ 　　　　　　　　　　　　**2.** $4 + {}^-3$

3. $7 - ({}^-1)$ 　　　　　　　　　　**4.** $^-2 - ({}^-1)$

5. $^-6 + 2$ 　　　　　　　　　　　　**6.** $10 - 8$

7. $^-10 - ({}^-5)$ 　　　　　　　　**8.** $6 + ({}^-2)$

9. $7 + 3$ 　　　　　　　　　　　　**10.** $^-5 - 3$

11   **Working with Integers**   **Exercise 73**

Lessons 11.1, 11.4 and 11.5

A. Compare. Use >, <, or =.

    1.   6 _____ ⁻6   **2.**   ⁻4 _____ ⁻3   **3.**   0 _____ 6

    4.   3 _____ 3   **5.**   ⁻1 _____ ⁻2   **6.**   0 _____ ⁻1

B. Add or subtract.

    1. $4 + {}^-3$ **2.** ${}^-8 - {}^-5$

    3. $18 + {}^-15$ **4.** ${}^-27 + 9$

    5. ${}^-14 - {}^-7$ **6.** $32 - {}^-16$

CRITICAL THINKING

Solve the problems.

    1.   Two deep-sea divers were 15 feet below sea level. Then they came up 10 feet. Were they still below the sea level? Explain using an expression.

    2.   John wants to buy a stereo for $200. His checking account has $192. What would his new balance be if he bought the stereo?

11 ▶ Multiplying Integers   Exercise 74

Lessons 11.2, 11.4, and 11.6

A. Write *true* or *false* after each sentence. If the sentence is
false, change the underlined word or words to make it true.

1. The sum of two positive integers is <u>always</u> positive.

_____

2. The product of two positive integers <u>is not</u> always positive.

_____

3. The absolute value of an integer is always <u>positive</u>.

_____

4. The product of a positive integer and a negative integer is <u>negative</u>.

_____

B. Find each product.

1. 2 ($^-$3)   **2.** 3 (1)

3. 4 ($^-$1)   **4.** ($^-$3) ($^-$2)

C. Circle the expression that is not equivalent.

1. (3) ($^-$2)

    a. ($^-$3) (2)   **b.** ($^-$2) (3)   **c.** (3) (2)

2. ($^-$4) ($^-$3)

    a. ($^-$4) (3)   **b.** ($^-$3) ($^-$4)   **c.** (4) (3)

3. (3) (6)

    a. ($^-$3) ($^-$6)   **b.** (6) (3)   **c.** ($^-$6) (3)

Dividing Integers Exercise 75

Lessons 11.6 and 11.7

A. Write *true* or *false* after each sentence. If the sentence is false, change the underlined word to make it true.

1. The quotient of two negative integers is <u>negative</u>.

_____

2. The quotient of a positive integer and a negative integer is <u>negative</u>.

_____

3. The quotient of two positive integers is <u>positive</u>.

_____

B. Write division facts to complete the table.

1. 2(3) = 6	6 ÷ 2 = 3	6 ÷ 3 = 2
2. 5(⁻2) = ⁻10		
3. (⁻2)(⁻6) = 12		
4. (⁻10)(3) = ⁻30		
5. (⁻12)(⁻3) = 36		

C. Divide. Use multiplication to check.

1. 15 ÷ 3

2. ⁻25 ÷ ⁻5

3. ⁻30 ÷ 6

4. 15 ÷ (⁻5)

5. ⁻48 ÷ 6

6. ⁻50 ÷ (⁻10)

11 ▶ Problem Solving Using Integers Exercise 76

Lessons 11.4 to 11.7

Circle the answer for each operation.

1. ⁻2 • 3
   a. ⁻6   **b.** ⁻5   **c.** ⁻1

2. ⁻5 + 6
   a. ⁻11   **b.** 1   **c.** ⁻1

3. (⁻6) (⁻9)
   a. 56   **b.** ⁻54   **c.** 54

4. ⁻16 ÷ 8
   a. 2   **b.** ⁻8   **c.** ⁻2

CRITICAL THINKING

Solve the problems.

1. Queen Elizabeth II may be the wealthiest woman in the world. One source said her wealth was $900 million. Another source said her wealth was $270 million. Find the difference.

2. The lowest point in the United States is in Death Valley. The depth is 86 meters below sea level. Mt. McKinley in Alaska is the highest point in the United States and has an altitude of 6,194 meters. What is the distance between the lowest point and the highest point?

3. The greatest temperature change in one day was recorded in Browning, Montana. The temperature changed from 44°F above zero to 56°F below zero. What was the change?

Name _____ Date _____

 Solving Problems Together Exercise 77

Lessons 11.9 and 11.10

Work with a partner to solve these problems.

1. How many different groups of 3 letters can you make from the word COAST?

2. Shani, Esti, Jeremy, Toby, Tara, and Barry are officers of the Math Club. Two of them must make phone calls to plan a meeting. How many different groups of two can be made from the six officers?

3. Mauna Kea, a mountain in Hawaii, measures 13,796 feet above sea level. But the mountain extends all the way to the ocean floor. The height of the mountain from the ocean floor is 33,480 feet. How much of the mountain is below sea level?

4. The longest mountain range is below sea level. It is called the Mid-Ocean Ridge. It has a length of 40,000 miles. The longest mountain range above sea level is in the Andes in South America. It is 4,700 miles long. How much longer is the range below sea level?

5. The Dead Sea in the Middle East is the deepest land area in the world. The surface is 1,310 feet below sea level. The deepest point in the bed of the Dead Sea is 3,875 feet below sea level. Find the difference.

12 ▶ Evaluating Expressions with Integers   Exercise 78

Lessons 12.1 and 12.2

A. Circle the equivalent expression.

1. $2y - (^-3)$

   a. $2y + 3$ **b.** $^-2y - 3$ **c.** $^-2y + 3$

2. $^-3x \div ^-2$

   a. $3x \div ^-2$ **b.** $3x \div 2$ **c.** $^-3x (^-2)$

3. $^-6 - 5a$

   a. $^-6 + (^-5a)$ **b.** $6 + 5a$ **c.** $^-6 + 5a$

4. $^-6 (^-8)$

   a. 14 **b.** $^-48$ **c.** 48

B. Complete the table.

Expression	$2x + 5$	$^-3a + 10$	$^-6(a + b)$	$6 - (^-3a)$
Value of:	$x = 6$	$a = ^-4$	$a = 3, b = ^-1$	$a = ^-2$
Substitution	$2(6) + 5$	$^-3(\_\_\_) + 10$	$^-6(\_\_\_ + \_\_\_)$	$6 - (^-3 \cdot \_\_\_)$
Substitution	$12 + 5$	$\_\_\_ + 10$	$^-6(\_\_\_)$	$6 - (\_\_\_)$
Value of expression	17			

C. Find the value.

1. $8 - 2a$ when $a = ^-2$ 2. $^-4 (2x + y)$ when $x = ^-5$ and $y = 3$

12 **Expressions with Integers** **Exercise 79**

Lessons 12.1 to 12.3, 12.6

A. Write *true* or *false* after each sentence. If the sentence is false, change the underlined word or words to make it true.

1. When you combine like terms, the variables of the combined terms must be <u>the same</u>.

   _____

2. When subtracting like terms with integers, rewrite subtraction as <u>multiplication</u>.

   _____

3. When you multiply both sides of an inequality by the same negative number, the inequality <u>does not</u> change.

   _____

B. Find the value of each expression if $a = {}^-1$, $b = 3$, and $c = 4$.

1. $a^2 - 2b$ 2. ${}^-a - b - c$ 3. ${}^-2b + 5c$

4. $b^2 - 4ac$ 5. $a^2 + b^2$ 6. $c - 4a$

CRITICAL THINKING

Solve the problem.

A good way to measure the value of a fitness program is to find your target heart rate. The expressions below give the target heart rate.

Males	.65(220 − Age)
Females	.65(225 − Age)

a. Find the target heart rate of a 16-year-old male.

b. Find the target heart rate of a 16-year-old female.

12 ▷ Solving Equations with Integers

Exercise 80

Lesson 12.3

Solve each equation. Then check your solution.

    1. $2x = 10$ **2.** $5x - 1 = 14$ **3.** $^{-}2x + 3 = 7$

    4. $5x + 1 = 6$ **5.** $^{-}x = {}^{-}5$ **6.** $3 = {}^{-}3 - x$

CRITICAL THINKING

Write an expression for each.

    1. The sum of two different numbers. _____

    2. The difference of two different numbers. _____

    3. The product of a number and 5. _____

    4. The sum of a number and 10. _____

Solve the problems.

    5. The perimeter of a garden is 600 feet. The width is 132 feet. Find the length. (Use $P = 2l + 2w$.)

    6. The difference in ticket prices for a concert is $18. The higher price ticket is $30. How much is the lower price ticket?

Name _____ Date _____

 12 ▶ **Graphing Inequalities**   **Exercise 81**

Lesson 12.4

A. Write *true* or *false* after each sentence. If the sentence is
false, change the underlined word to make it true.

1. You can graph the <u>solution</u> of an equation on the number line.

   _____

2. The solution to $x > 2$ is all the numbers to the <u>left</u> of 2 on the number line.

   _____

3. The solution to $x < {}^{-}3$ is all the numbers to the <u>right</u> of ${}^{-}3$ on the number line.

   _____

B. Draw and label a number line for each problem. Then
graph the inequality.

   1. $x \geq 4$ 2. $a < 5$ 3. $y \geq {}^{-}2$

   4. $b < 0$ 5. $r \leq 0$ 6. $t \geq {}^{-}4$

C. Draw and label a number line. Graph each pair of
inequalities on the same number line.

   1. $x > 4$ 2. $x < {}^{-}3$
      $x < 4$ $x > {}^{-}3$

Solving Inequalities Using Addition and Subtraction

Exercise 82

Lesson 12.5

A. Write *true* or *false*.

1. $0 > 0$ _____

2. $^-400 > ^-2$ _____

3. $^-5 < ^-5$ _____

4. $8 > ^-8$ _____

5. $^-18 < ^-10$ _____

6. $0 < ^-6$ _____

7. $10 < ^-15$ _____

8. $x < 6$ means the same as $6 < x$ _____

B. Solve each inequality. Graph the solution.

1. $x - 3 < 2$

2. $a + 4 \geq 5$

3. $b + 4 \geq 10$

4. $x - 5 < ^-2$

5. In Problem 1 above, name some values for x that make your inequality true. (Use your graph.)

6. In Problem 1 above, name some values for x that make your inequality false. (Use your graph.)

Problem Solving Using Integers and Algebra

Exercise 83

Lessons 12.2, 12.3, and 12.8

Use <, >, or =. Let x = 5 and y = ‾2.

1. $x + 2$ _____ 6

2. $x - 3$ _____ ‾5

3. $x + 2$ _____ ‾6

4. $x - 3$ _____ 5

5. $x - y$ _____ 3

6. $x - 7$ _____ y

CRITICAL THINKING

Solve the problems.

1. Mario scored 92 on a math test. Kay's score was 3 points different from Mario's. What was Kay's score? (There are two answers.)

2. Last week, Sophia worked 10 hours longer than Robbie worked. Together, they worked 62 hours. How many hours did they each work?

3. The lowest temperature in Garrison was ‾18°F. The highest temperature was 97°F. Find the range.

12 ➤ **Finding Probability**   **Exercise 84**

Lesson 12.9

Work with a partner or in a group to find the probabilities.

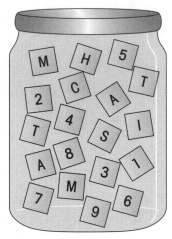

1. Find the probability of selecting a number.

2. Find the probability of selecting a letter.

3. Find the probability of selecting an even number.

4. Find the probability of selecting a prime number.

5. Find the probability of selecting a number divisible by 3.

6. Find the probability of selecting a consonant letter.

7. Find the probability of selecting an A.

8. Find the probability of selecting a letter that is not a consonant.

9. Write three questions of your own about probabilities.

    a. _____

    _____

    b. _____

    _____

    c. _____

    _____

Date _____

13 ▸ Ordered Pairs   Exercise 85

Lessons 13.1 and 13.2

A. Fill in the lines. Write *right* or *left*, and *up,* or *down*.

   1. (3, 5) move _____ 3 and _____ 5.

   2. ($^-$2, 4) move _____ 2 and _____ 4.

   3. ($^-$1, $^-$3) move _____ 1 and _____ 3.

   4. (0, $^-$5) move _____ 0 and _____ 5.

   5. (0, 0) move _____ 0 and _____ 0.

B. Give the ordered pair for each.

   1. Move right 4 and move up 5. _____.

   2. Move left 3 and move up 6. _____.

   3. Move left 5 and move down 2. _____.

   4. Move right 2 and move down 3. _____.

   5. Move right 0 and move down 2. _____.

C. On the coordinate plane, give the location of each point. Write the letter of each point on the line.

   1. A at (5, 4)

   2. B at ($^-$2, 3)

   3. C at (0, 5)

   4. D at ($^-$4, $^-$2)

   5. E at (2, $^-$4)

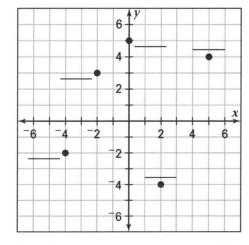

Chapter 13 • The Coordinate Plane   85

13 ▶ **Coordinate Axes**   **Exercise 86**

Lessons 13.1 and 13.2

A. Write *true* or *false* after each sentence. If the sentence is false, change the underlined word to make it true.

  1. A coordinate plane has two <u>perpendicular</u> number lines.

  _____

  2. The horizontal number line is called the <u>*y*-axis</u>.

  _____

  3. The vertical number line is called the <u>*x*-axis</u>.

  _____

B. Draw coordinate axes. Graph and label each point.

  1. A at (2, 0)

  2. B at (⁻3, 1)

  3. C at (4, ⁻2)

  4. D at (⁻2, ⁻2)

  5. E at (0, 4)

  6. F at (0, 0)

  7. G at (⁻2, ⁻4)

  8. H at (4, 2)

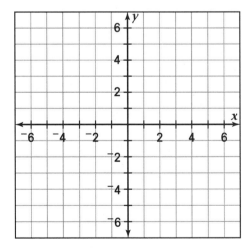

Name _____ Date _____

13 ▶ Graphing Equations   **Exercise 87**

Lessons 13.3 and 13.4

A. Complete each table.

1.

x	⁻2	⁻1	0	1	2
$y = 2x - 1$					

2.

x	⁻2	⁻1	0	1	2
$y = {}^-3x + 1$					

3.

x	⁻2	⁻1	0	1	2
$y = 5 - 2x$					

B. Graph each equation in Section A.

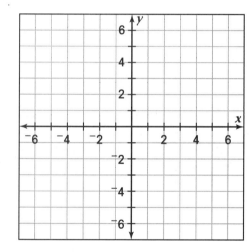

13 ▸ Using Patterns of Ordered Pairs to Determine Equations

Exercise 88

Lesson 13.3

A. Circle the ordered pair that makes each equation true.

1. $y = 3x - 2$

    a. $(0, 1)$ **b.** $(^-1, ^-5)$ **c.** $(2, 8)$

2. $y = ^-x$

    a. $(^-2, ^-2)$ **b.** $(0, 0)$ **c.** $(1, 1)$

3. $y = ^-2x - 1$

    a. $(^-1, ^-3)$ **b.** $(0, 1)$ **c.** $(^-1, 1)$

4. $y = x + 3$

    a. $(0, 3)$ **b.** $(^-3, ^-6)$ **c.** $(4, 1)$

CRITICAL THINKING

B. Find the equation for each set of ordered pairs. Circle the answer.

1. $(0, 0)$ $(^-3, ^-3)$ $(5, 5)$

    a. $y = 3x + 2$ **b.** $y = x$ **c.** $y = ^-2x - 1$

2. $(0, 1)$ $(1, 5)$ $(^-2, ^-7)$

    a. $y = ^-2x + 1$ **b.** $y = ^-x$ **c.** $y = 4x + 1$

3. $(1, 2)$ $(3, 4)$ $(5, 6)$

    a. $y = x + 1$ **b.** $y = ^-4x$ **c.** $y = 3x - 2$

4. $(0, 0)$ $(1, 2)$ $(^-3, ^-6)$

    a. $y = ^-x + 4$ **b.** $y = 2x$ **c.** $y = 4x$

Name _____ Date _____

13 ▸ Graphing Equations from Patterns of Ordered Pairs

Exercise 89

Lessons 13.3 and 13.4

A. Fill in the lines. Then graph each equation.

1. $y = 2x + 5$

If $x = 2$, then $y = $ _____

If $x = {}^-1$, then $y = $ _____

If $x = 0$, then $y = $ _____

2. $y = {}^-x - 5$

If $x = 2$, then $y = $ _____

If $x = {}^-1$, then $y = $ _____

If $x = 0$, then $y = $ _____

3. $y = {}^-1 + x$

If $x = 2$, then $y = $ _____

If $x = {}^-1$, then $y = $ _____

If $x = 0$, then $y = $ _____

4. $y = 4 - 3x$

If $x = 2$, then $y = $ _____

If $x = {}^-1$, then $y = $ _____

If $x = 0$, then $y = $ _____

B. Use graph paper. Graph each equation. Use values of x: ${}^-2$, 0, 2.

1. $y = 2x + 5$

2. $y = 4 - 2x$

3. $y = x - 4$

4. $y = 3 + 2x$

5. $y = {}^-2x + 5$

13 ▶ Using a Line Graph

Lesson 13.6

Use the line graph to answer the questions. Describe the points with ordered pairs.

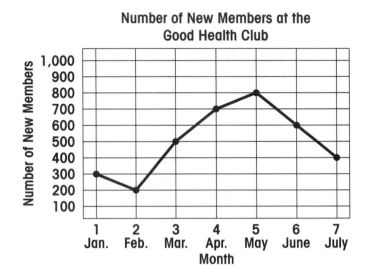

Number of New Members at the Good Health Club

1. Which month had the highest number of new members?

2. Which month had the lowest number of new members?

3. Which month had half the number of new members that May had?

4. Which month had twice the number of new members that January had?

5. Which month had 300 more new members than the previous month?

Finding the Slope of the Line   **Exercise 91**

Lesson 13.7

On the coordinate plane, draw two lines. Locate two points
on each line. Record the ordered pairs for these points. Ask
a classmate to find the slope of each line.

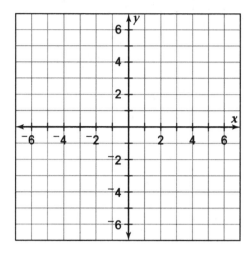

1. What is the slope of the line that contains (_____ , _____)
    and (_____ , _____)?

2. What is the slope of the line that contains (_____ , _____)
    and (_____ , _____)?

CRITICAL THINKING

Locate two more points on the first line. Use these points to
find the slope. Is this slope the same as the one you found
in number **1**? Explain.